Business Triumph Keys

Keys

DR A. J. AJENGBE

DEDICATION

To God Almighty.

CONTENTS

ACKNOWLEDGMENTS

My appreciations go to everyone who made this work a success.

Preface

The dream of every business man is to become successful in business. Failure is an eye saw, so no one wants to experience failure either temporarily or permanently in his endeavor. There is saying that "failure is not failure, but failure to learn from failure is".

Though some school of thought believe that there is no magical key to business success, but experience has revealed that it is pertinent that entrepreneurs work hard both on the organizational and intellectual levels of their businesses to attract success into their lives.

Simply put, successful entrepreneurs are those who overcome both subjective and objective hurdles.

Understanding that the world is rapidly changing, this special book guides you into business triumphant keys that can help you conquer and succeed in life and business.

Happy reading!

Introduction

Business is any venture you engage in that earns you income. Whether you are in paid employment or self-employment or in big time business, we all are in business. I want you to see that job or a business and I will tell you why you got that job because you are suitably qualified for it. You have your first degree, first leaving school certificate, WASSCE, National Diploma, NCE, a Bachelor's degree, Master's degree, professional qualification etc. a lot of money have gone into it. The reason you don't know is because a large part of it was done by your parents or benefactors and you got a lighter part of it wait till you have children, then you know a lot of money has gone into training your children. Please, note your children are your life investment, take it or leave it. So, parenting is big time business. Your capital in that job is your years of financial, behavioral, social and time investment in the acquisition of knowledge, skills and certification. So, you now see why you don't joke on your job. When many people are jubilating that they got job they have not carved out a path to make the most of their investment on the job, that's why many don't get promoted on the job.

In Nigeria, take business as a second option when they are unable to land a job and you begin to wonder who created those jobs. Your guess is as right as mine, the government. We rely on the government for everything, in the west, the richest people are business people but in Africa the riches are politicians and corrupt government officials. That is why government jobs looks very lucrative and attractive. even the budget shows 70% recurrent and 30% capital meaning you will fund government expenses with 70% why won'tpeople drift into government jobs and even the 30% for business may not get into the hands of business people but imagine if the reverse is the case, then many public servants would have come into business. It is succinct to classify business

- self-employment: you and at most 2 people

- micro business : 1-10

- small: 11-100

- medium: 101-300

- large: 301 and above

Whatever is your level right now the aim of this book is to move you gradually from being self-employed, micro, small, medium into a large business. I will release 12 keys of business growth into your and these may not be Harvard business school model but they are keys that will work if all you learnt in Harvard, Yale, Caltech, UI, Ife or ABU failed. These principles are rugged; they can breakthrough any obstacle, they are also applicable by people of different tribes or religion. These are:

- Knowledge And Wisdom

- Meditation And Planning

- Purity

- Faith

- Hope

- Prayers

- Speaking In Tongues

- Perseverance

- Giving

- The Anointing

- Confession

Chapter 1

Knowledge And Wisdom

it is important to distinguish between knowledge and wisdom,

What is knowledge? It is the acquisition of skills, facts or standards in a certain field or department of life. Knowledge is the know what. It means to be aware but awareness is not equal to performance.

What is wisdom? It is the correct application of knowledge. it is the knowhow. Not just knowing what to do, but how to go about it. As a business manger, I know the differences between efficiency and effectiveness. similarly, there is a wide world of difference between knowledge and wisdom.

The reason many are not succeeding in business is because they know next to nothing in their filed or business.

You need adequate knowledge in your business. Get relevant literatures in your chosen field of endeavor. Invest in books, articles, journals that are relevant to your subject. If truly you want to excel in that business then your library must have more literature on that subject right now because if you know more then you can do more. See people say knowledge is power, knowledge is light. So, with knowledge that powerlessness that have stagnated you in business will disappear.

However, many times you find out that there is little variation between knowledge you acquired and the real life situation. That is the place of wisdom. Haven't you wondered two individuals who went through the same institution and acquired same kind of training but one became successful in that same vocation and the other couldn't find his feet?

Even the holy Bible said wisdom is the principal thing that is wisdom is the main thing in life. If you major on the major then you end up as a major player. There is a wisdom path for successful business in any environment.

Vision

What is vision? It is the plan or end result of anything. Vision is the ultimate goal set out for any vocation, project, life or a people. Vision is not some midnight script or a movie playing in front of you. It is a mental picture which defines your physical posture in life.

Why is vision important?

- without it life or business is aimless. without aims achievement is not in view

- it brings tomorrow to today

- it pumps energy into you. doubt and confusion about such matter becomes minimized

- it is a fuel for accomplishment. anytime you look at your vision written or mental your energy level rises and it positions you for accomplishment

- it is imaginative in nature: success is about 90% mental and 10% physical in communication

- many business are struggling because of visionlessness

- What is your vision for the business you are running, even our nation had to roll out an economic recovery growth plan(ERGP) by the days government

Characteristics Of Vision

- Your vision is long term but can be broken into shorter terms which are called goals. That is why I always ask business people if they are in business to play or for business? You see, that multibillion naira Vision Empire of yours should be broken into yearly, monthly, weekly, even daily goals. These goals must be congruent with your vision. goals are short term or medium term. Don't let ideas deceive you. It is in planning that you segmentize your idea and channel the dos and don'ts. You must have a planning time, usually after prayer I engage in 1 hour plan. Don't just rush with your idea you may get stranded on the way take out time to plan

- Write down everything: Some people think their brain is supersonic so they don't write but research has shown that writing down your ideas is about 30% contribution to success. Writing does not only connote pen and paper. You may use your smart phones, laptops or desktops. Just write so that you can crystallize your vision.

• Use your mind: Imagination is powerful. It is the creation of an image in your mind and most time you see it happening around you. When I read the book think and grow rich. I discovered how powerful the brain was and how most people including i have abandoned it to reflexes. now, your business is simply crulling because you lack ideas. Ideas they say rule the world. People of ideas are always resourceful and progressive. YOU MUST COMMIT TO THE USE OF YOUR MIND IN BUSINESS you have competitors, you need to be ahead of them and that is brain work. Since I read the book "think and grow rich" I have berated physical labor, the main stuff is mental. It is dangerous to be mental lack. That's why you must read a lot. A business person must know more than a university professor because while the professor teaches a handful of students per time, the business man has the whole world as his client base. Show me a striving business man and I will show you a avid reader. They have good books in their library. The poor sleep more than the rich. See a rich man awake all night but poor people with poverty mentality sleep 10pm-6am the next day wasting 1/3 of his day on productive ventures. You are sleeping too much. Your business is not working well. Wake up in the night and read relevant books, read journals, magazines, articles that can enhance your knowledge. A struggling businessman sleep all night, why won't his business sleep!

Learn from experts, people who have proofs of success in business.

• Challenges: challenges they say is the food of champions. Your vision will be challenged, am just being real. At some point you feel like what am I doing here? Let me throw in the towel but don't. Why? You have invested time, energy, resources into that business so why back out suddenly; it may just amount to waste. Get ready for daunting challenging, they are normally there to make your story complete but if you redress then that will amount to failure. Tell yourself even if I fail, I refuse to quit. Failure is a blessing in disguise. Research has shown that most outstanding success failed seven times before it finally succeeded. That's quite informative for you. When you fail learn your lesson and move on because there is future ahead of you, which you cannot jeopardize.

• Association: Your thought will affect your association and your association will affect your lifestyle. Check those you associating with, are they going anywhere at all what do you discuss most. Your association determines your allocation. Watch out for unfriendly friends and visionless people, let it not even affect who to marry. I don't see why you want to marry a lady or a guy who doesn't want to do business and you are into business. It won't work.

Don't allow anybody to distract you from your goal and waste your entire life. Rather, attract people and those who are like minded. Now I have discovered too many drawbacks with organizations and business.

- Communication

- Leadership

Many business people know where they are going but their employees are not in the picture of it. If you want your business to do well, learn to dominate the vision and goals and sell it to your employees, well written on the tablets of their heart with adequate understanding.

Similarly, the owner doesn't appear to the people as a serious minded person, the body language just depicts they just come to get their own piece of cake . That is the pollution from the Nigerian public service; no performance indicator.

You want a thriving business then you need good leadership and communication skills.

Chapter 2

Meditation and planning

What is meditation?

Meditation is an act of reasoning or thinking through an idea or analysis of one. A Goodman said "if you think enough what you have is enough" meditation is something missing in this generation. They do everything but not meditation. That's why success is scarce, you see them sweating and wasting on something that good thinking and planning will sharply put in their hands. Meditation is the hearth of innovation and creativity and there is element of a thriving career or business.

The power of an idea

Many people ask what an idea is. An idea is not just doing a new thing but doing old things in a new way.

An idea is:

- An insight

- A light

- An inspiration

- A better perspective

- An answer

- A result of enquiry

- A product of intuition

You might have heard countless times that ideas rule the world that's the essence of this section.

Anything, systems, methods, people, business, governments attracted as an idea. Before you were born, your parents had an idea of having a child and they sprang into action an you came forth. The most dreaded thing that can happen to a man on earth is ignorance or simply put lack of awareness or idea. It will amaze you that the clothe you are wearing is an individual ideas. When you have idea you dictate the pace. When you have idea you shine. You rule, you control others, you dominate. A Chineese proverb said" the world will make a way for anyone who knows where he is going."

Simply put, its about one who has an idea. The young man that gave Coca-Cola the idea to package their products into bottles kissed poverty bye for life, he and his entire lineage. An idea did it for him. Look at Bill Gates, see what an idea did for this young man. In Africa, that is different especially in Nigeria we love physical labor-carry heavy loads panting like an Olympic athlete who just won a marathon. We don't have mental laborers. The reason I'm talking like this is because you are an entrepreneur and I want your business to outlive you. Your major duty is mental than your employees can go ahead and do the physical stuff and get paid. There are a lot of facilities he government put in place to spur entrepreneurship but where is the entrepreneurship skills to access and utilize them efficiently and effectively. We are in recession technically because the private sector is weak.

But as great as an idea may be if it's not subjected to critical and purposeful thinking, it may not maximize result; that the place of meditation. You meditate and ruminate on the ideas till it begins to manifest.

How to make meditation work for business growth

- Always enquire to know what, why, where and how a condition or things work
- How do we improve on it
- Are there better alternatives

Because where there is no enquiry there can be no discovery

Purity

Purity talks of cleanliness, probity, integrity. You can't be doing business in deception and cruelty and expect growth. A customer you deceive today can lead to the loss of about 120 others them check the multiplier effect of each of the 120 telling their own 120 people to do business with you. Don't cheat and ground your business because of momentary of temporary gains.

Let your hands be clean. Do clean business especially

that you fear God and build loyalty and trust in people. A good name is better than silver and gold.

If you keep doing business faithfully and truthfully there will be a time you will make it and that growth will be steady. Don't cheat people in a bid to increase business in that way are actually destroying your business. As you may have discovered your business is about people which means no people, no business. In the hierarchy of wealth, relationship is higher than cash. They are 7 of them, it's important you know them and re-orient you're your lifestyle to maximal profiting knowing and doing what matters most.

Chapter 3

Faith

What is faith

- Faith is knowing the will of God and following the way to actualizing it

- Faith is sharing responsibility with God in the light of scriptures so as to have your desire delivered

So faith is not just a belief or hope, it is a lifestyle is an act. But your faith in God will answer based on your standing with God. Who you are to god will determine what happens to you.

What to note about faith

- It is of a religious logic or sectional terminology

- Faith is not a gamble

- Faith is a tool of spiritual battle

- Faith is the only connecting rod between the natural and supernatural

- Faith puts you in command of situation and circumstances of life. In the very class of God.

- Faith works or doest based o your walk with God

- Faith is a heavy weight virtue

Why faith in business

Many people don't even have faith in and the workings of their business. In faith you have a responsibility-work study, prayers, fellowship and communion with the holy spirit etc. faith is a personal responsibility meaning one man's faith cannot answer for another, it is your "your faith that will make you whole'. You need faith in business because

- It helps to rule in the world of impossibilities

- Faith affects animate and inanimate object

- Faith is an evidence of answered prayers

- It builds expectation and hope which is critical to receiving
- It motivates you to believe in God, people and yourself and by so doing you are unstoppable

Characteristics of faith

- It is a seeking force
- It is a driving force
- It is a restful force
- It is a daring force
- It is an ever wining force

Start speaking sales, growth, and enlargement into your business. You have been with those goods or properties for days, weeks. Speak sales into it. Tell it to behave and have faith in God. If you ask in such a manner and do not doubt in your heart then your miracle is sure.

One unique thing about faith is that it gives a cheque in prayers and in the financial world a cheque is equivalent to cash.

Hope

What is hope?

Hope is expectation of a better outcome. It is futuristic. Expectation is the mother of manifestation and what you don't expect you cannot experience.

Hope is what will keep you going in the face of opposition and resistances to your progress. But it is important to note that it is faith that fuels hope in a business person. Hope makes you keep seeking opportunities to make the most of your adventures and reaching your goal. Hope is the light that makes the assurances that something will turn in your favor which eventually will do. Hope keeps your expectation alive but since your expectation determines your experience then hope will make your experience a glorious one.

Ways to fan your hope

- Always have a vision written and regularly reviewed
- Keep company with hopeful people

- Be open to new information and technologies: it will keep your mind fresh and sharpen your vision

- Always have flexible plans

- Focus on results not obstacles

- B an impulsive thinker

- Be a team payer

DR A. J. AJENGBE

Chapter 4

Prayers

Every individual, people pray irrespective of religion, sex, color, race or status. There is a natural consciousness that there is a supreme authority that is above all . I perceive as a reader you belong to a region.

You see, the dynamism and volatility of business makes it pertinent to engage in prayers. Remember that you are not the only one doing business there are lots of people so there is a risk factor, that's why you seek a higher power to help you which is God. You can get books on prayer especially my book on praying and praying through for further reference.

Speaking in tongues

It is otherwise called praying in the spirit. It is common knowledge that the spiritual controls and influence the physical. Your spiritual buoyancy will have a direct role on your business, life and well being.

It is succinct to note that you can pray in knowledge and you can do that in the spirit. People resort to this sort of prayers when they sense that they need higher help from above.

Why should you speak in tongues?

- Satanic forces are spiritual while you see their physical effect but if you want to fight back you engage in a spiritual fight
- It edifies you
- It is a secured medium of spiritual communication
- Puts you in the place of dominion
- Supernatural fruitfulness and enlargement is established
- Hunger for the things of God
- A good stimulant in prayers

Chapter 5

The Price Of Perseverance

Perseverance means endurance, persistence, unrelenting in a given task. It is an ever give up tonic from your inside until your business becomes a global success.

Many people give in and sellout, just a few days to breakthrough, they give up and throw in the towel. Friends, you are closer to success than where you have started. Research has shown that outstanding successes usually failed at least 7times.

I remembered vividly the story of Benjamin Franklyn who failed elections severally but finally became American president. Look at our dear president, Muhammadu Bahari who failed elections for 16 years but finally the made it in 2015. Can you imagine if he didn't contest in 2015, he would have missed it in history.

The gift of Giving

As a business person there are different platforms to give

- Tithing
- Offerings
- Corporate social responsibility
- Taxation

I will technically focus on CSR and Taxation

There are many businesses evading and avoiding tax and so they don't even engage in CSR. Remember without the society your business and you can't exist. Remit your taxes, give back to the society also engage in religious giving. This is what they practice in the west, that is, why their businesses keep going well and profiting.

Chapter 6

The Anointing

The anointing is the divine enabling. It is divine help, divine grace, and divine ability. Your business is destined to be great and loaded but you will not explode without the anointing. Without the anointing you cannot break forth and manifest what God has loaded inside of you. Remember, your well being is the well being of your business. If you suffer spiritual defect, it will show in your business

Have the anointing

- To rule and reign in the midst of your enemy
- To open up your destiny
- To preserve and sustain progress
- To scale new heights-change levels

- For empowerment

The anointing of the Holy Spirit is for all spheres of human endeavor. The more anointed you are the more the breakthrough you command. Your level or profitability is anointing dependent.

How to encounter the anointing

- Righteous living
- Genuine thirst
- Pray for it
- Look for men who have it and follow them
- Humility

Note that anointing is the digging of hands of god in the life of a man.

The power of confession

What you say determines what you see. You can't be confessing hardship and expect a flourishing business. In this part of the world, it is normal or termed humility to complain and that's why many issues are complicated here. Keep saying good things about your business and you see it taking shape. Confession is very powerful; it creates your desired future. Words are every powerful, it is one of the strongest armory in spiritual warfare

Wakeup at night and early in the morning and say what you want to see and you keep changing from glory to glory.

About The Author

Dr A. J. Ajengbe is the GMD/CEO of Ajengbe Group a conglomerate that comprises: Jengbens Global Concept limited, Pearls Associates Financial services, Ajengbe Publications, Global Mission education Centre and Sunday Emmanuel Ajengbe Memorial Foundation.